God Makes a Way

© 2022 by TGS International, a wholly owned subsidiary of Christian Aid Ministries, Berlin, Ohio.

All rights reserved. No part of this book may be reproduced or stored in any retrieval system, in any form or by any means, electronic or mechanical, without written permission from the publisher except for brief quotations embodied in critical articles and reviews.

ISBN: 978-1-63813-082-6

Cover and text layout design: Kristi Yoder

Illustrated by Igor Kondratyuk

Printed in China

Published by:
TGS International
P.O. Box 355
Berlin, Ohio 44610 USA
Phone: 330.893.4828
Fax: 330.893.4893
www.tgsinternational.com

God Makes a Way

Melissa Wingard

Illustrated by Igor Kondratyuk

"Cock-a-doodle-doo!" The rooster's morning wake-up call was followed by a steady *drip, drip, plink; drip, drip, plink.*

Sleepily Faith rubbed her eyes. When "Two Feet," their pet rooster, hollered "Cock-a-doodle-doo" again a few minutes later, six-year-old Faith knew it was time to get up. She needed to go for water so she could take a bath before going to school.

Faith heard the *drip, drip, plink* of the dripping rain and then the soft snoring of her seven-year-old sister Rebecca on the mat beside her. She shook Rebecca's arm. "Rebecca!" Her sister just mumbled and rolled over. "REBECCA! Where's the flashlight? I'm going for water."

Rebecca felt the mat beside her until she found the flashlight. She clicked it on. A beam of light shot through the early morning darkness and Faith grabbed the flashlight. "Thank you o."

After Faith got dressed, she picked up her bucket and slid her feet into a pair of plastic slippers. She reached for the bent nail that served as a lock for the wooden door and shoved it down. The door swung open.

Cold raindrops hit her skin as she walked through the village. *Drip. Plink. Drip.* She shivered in the cool air of the Liberian morning. The day was now brightening, and when she got to the well some of her friends were already there, drawing water. Faith's "Good morning o" was greeted with a chorus of happy "Morning o's!"

A few more raindrops plinked from the sky and then stopped. Faith had just sat down on the concrete ledge beside her friend Sarah when Rebecca arrived and handed her the lapa[1] she had forgotten at the house. "Thank you, Rebecca," Faith said. Her ma often reminded them to be polite, even to their siblings.

---

[1] A piece of cloth designed to be worn as a wrap-around skirt, but in Africa it has many uses.

"Faith, you next," someone said. Faith jumped up and hurried to the pump. She did not want to miss her turn. She put her bucket under the spout and climbed up on the concrete ledge to reach the handle. *Crreeaakkk, sccrreech,* the pump complained as Faith worked the handle up and down. Faith listened for the comforting sound of water splashing into her bucket because that meant there was water. Her mother said one year the well ran dry and they had to walk for an hour to get water.

"It's full!" Sarah proclaimed loudly and Faith stopped pumping. She wound her lapa into a circle and placed it on her head. Then Sarah helped her balance the full bucket on her head.

"I will see you at school, Sarah," said Faith.

"Okay o," replied Sarah as Faith started back to her house.

When Faith reached home, everyone was awake. "Ma, may I have a few coals to make hot water?"

"No, Faith. There's only a little coal left, and we need that to cook our food today."

Faith looked disappointed. That meant she would have to take her bath with cold water. Quickly she gathered her ball of homemade soap, her school uniform, and her bucket of water before heading to the tin structure where they took their baths. Her stomach rumbled with hunger. She hoped Ma could sell some things from her garden today so there would be rice to eat when she came home from school.

Clean and dressed in her uniform, Faith put the bucket back into her room. She carried her black shoes outside where she wiped them with a rag so they would be shiny and clean. Her teacher was not happy when they came to school with dirty shoes or a wrinkled uniform. Copybook and pencil in hand, she sat down on a small wooden bench to wait for her sister.

Soon Rebecca came from behind the house and they set off down the dirt road to school. At school, all the classes lined up in the yard for prayer before being dismissed to their classrooms.

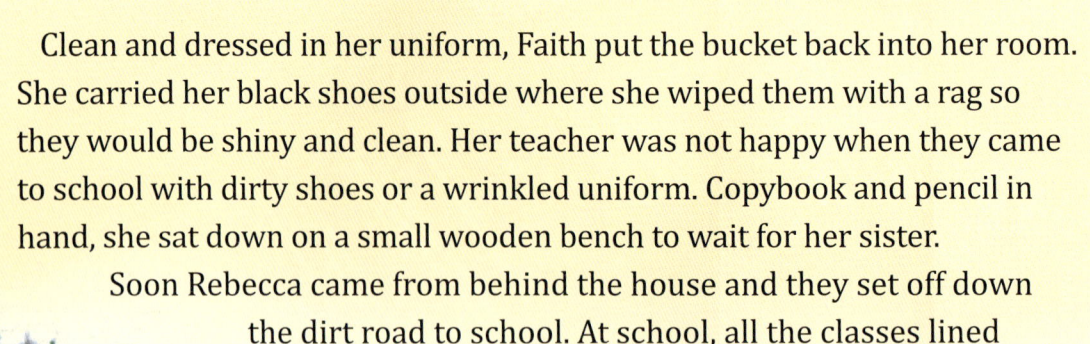

Faith put her copybook on her wooden desk and looked over at Sarah with a grin. She enjoyed everything about school. "Good morning, class," said the teacher.

"Good morning, teacher!" Faith and her classmates replied loudly. Miss Johnson smiled and began flipping through a book on her desk. She picked up her pencil. "Time for roll call. Abraham Jones?"

"Here!" shouted Abraham, jumping up from his seat. Miss Johnson looked at him sternly, and Abraham sank back into his chair with a sheepish grin. As Miss Johnson called out the names of her students, Faith waited eagerly until she heard "Faith Jomah?" She sat up straight and answered, "Here."

In a few minutes, roll call was finished. Miss Johnson picked up a piece of chalk and began to make a giant letter on the chalkboard.

"Okay, class, today we will be learning the letter 'I.' You make one straight line just like a tall man. Make sure he stands straight and tall! Then you make one line at the bottom so he has something to stand on. Then you give him a piece of rattan to carry on his head." Faith watched carefully because she wanted to do it just like Miss Johnson.

"Now I want everyone to find a clean page in your copybook and make I's. When you finish, lay down your pencil," instructed Miss Johnson. Carefully Faith began filling her page with capital I's.

Miss Johnson walked between the desks, carrying her rattan stick in case anyone misbehaved. After a few minutes Faith laid down her pencil, and Miss Johnson came to inspect her work. The teacher scrawled "Good" across the top and Faith smiled. *Ma will be happy,* she thought.

Soon the bell clanged and everyone jumped up from their seats and rushed through the door. Faith watched wistfully as Sarah handed recess money to Mercy, who was carrying a bucket of doughnuts on her head. Carefully Mercy wrapped one in a torn piece of paper and handed it to Sarah.

Faith could almost taste the sweet, fried dough. Her stomach rumbled again. And then, to Faith's surprise, Sarah tore off part of her doughnut and handed it to her. Faith almost danced with excitement. "Thank you, Sarah!" she exclaimed.

The two girls joined in a kickball game with their friends as they took bites of the sugar-crusted treat. All too soon the bell was clanging again. Faith licked the last bit of grease and sugar from her fingers. "Race you to the class," she told Sarah and took off running. Sarah was hard at her heels.

Faith and her class recited their 123s and practiced writing the numbers from one to ten. Before they went home, Miss Johnson told a story of a tortoise and a hare who had a race. "If you want to succeed," she told them, "think about the tortoise. Never, ever give up!"

Faith and her friends made plans to play lapa ball as they walked down the road toward home. They all raced home to change out of their school uniforms and then gathered in Faith's yard.

Faith took her lapa and wadded it into a ball. Everyone placed their slippers on a pile in the middle, and then they picked Sarah to go first. Faith and Favor giggled as they heaved the ball back and forth, trying to hit Sarah. She kept dodging the ball while trying to put the pile of slippers into pairs. Faith and her friends played and played until the sweat beaded on their cheeks and their empty stomachs forced them to stop. Hungrily they headed for home.

Faith walked to the kitchen behind the house, expecting to see Ma bent over a cooking fire. But there was no fire. *Where is Ma?* she wondered. Quickly she lifted the lid from the cooking pot to see if the rice was ready. But there was no rice—only a few small pieces of yam. *Did Ma go to buy food?*

Faith ran into the house. "Ma!" she called. "Where are you?" When Ma came from her room, Faith asked, "Ma, where's the rice? I'm hungry!"

"I am sorry, Faith, there is no more rice. And the money will not reach. But I found a small yam today, and I will cook it now."

Faith's shoulders drooped. Her stomach was so empty. The doughnut she and Sarah had shared at recess was long gone. She remembered the time she had gone to bed without eating. She hadn't slept well that night. Would it happen again? Faith felt a tear wanting to slip from her eye, but she tried to be brave. She did not want Ma to see her cry.

Ma slipped her arm around Faith's shoulders and squeezed. "Don't cry. When God is ready to do something, He will do it. Remember the time you were sick?" Faith rested her head against Ma and nodded. She liked when Ma told this story.

Faith looked up at her. "Can you tell me again?"

Ma turned Faith toward the door. "Come. I will tell you while I cook the yam." They went outside to the kitchen and Faith sat on her little wooden chair while Ma sent Rebecca to the neighbors for some hot coals to start the fire.

"Faith, before you were born I got sick. I don't know where I got it, but it is a sickness that doesn't go away. Even now we can't tell people that we have it, because they would be afraid and would not buy the things I am selling. Before you were born, the midwife said I would have to feed you with formula. I knew that would be expensive, and I didn't have enough money to buy it. Finally I decided, 'I have to trust God. He will make a way.' I have one friend who knows about our problem, so I asked her if she would help. She said she would help us get enough formula to feed you."

Soon Rebecca returned, carrying the hot coals on an old piece of tin. Faith watched as Ma made a hollow in the charcoal for the hot coals and then blew softly on them to start the fire. Soon smoke was curling upward.

"The night you were born it was storming and raining heavily. You were so beautiful with your head full of dark hair. You cried a lot that night because we didn't have food for you, but as soon as morning came, I got some formula. You ate well that day!"

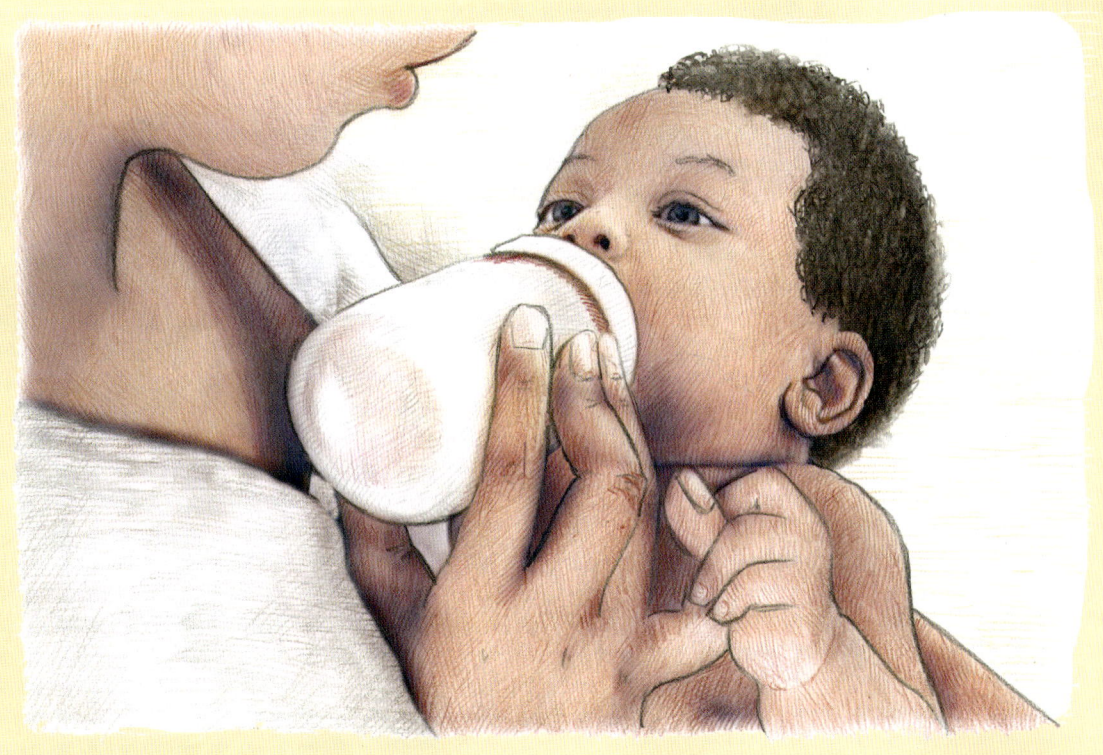

Ma put the pot with the yam on the cooking fire and continued, "We could see you were a healthy girl. You were growing and I hoped and prayed you would not be sick. But I was afraid you were. I didn't know what I would do with another sick child. I prayed and prayed that you would be healthy. After a few months my friend asked if you had been checked for the sickness. I told her I was too scared.

" 'But I think it would be good to know,' she said. 'Remember how Rebecca almost died before we knew about the sickness? We don't want that to happen again. Now she can take medicine and it helps her stay healthy. It would be good to know if Faith needs medicine too.' I knew she was right, but still I was afraid."

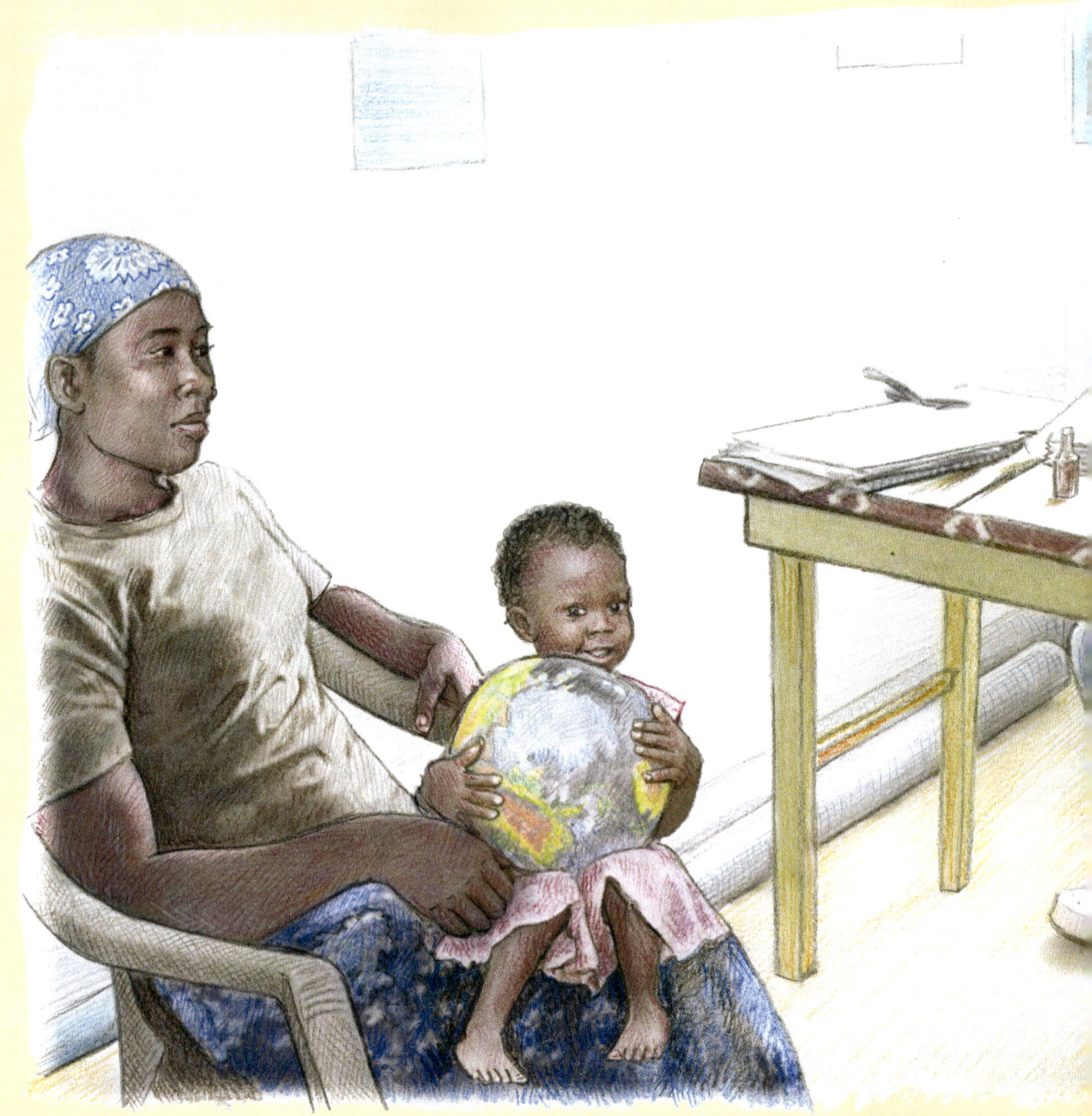

"The morning I took you to the hospital, my friend called to tell me she would be praying. I was praying too. When they told me you had the sickness too, I cried. A kind lady at the hospital saw how upset I was and said she would take you and raise you. I didn't know what to do. I called my friend and cried. I told her I was going to leave you with the lady at the hospital. She begged me not to do that. She kept saying, 'God will make a way. I know He will make a way.'"

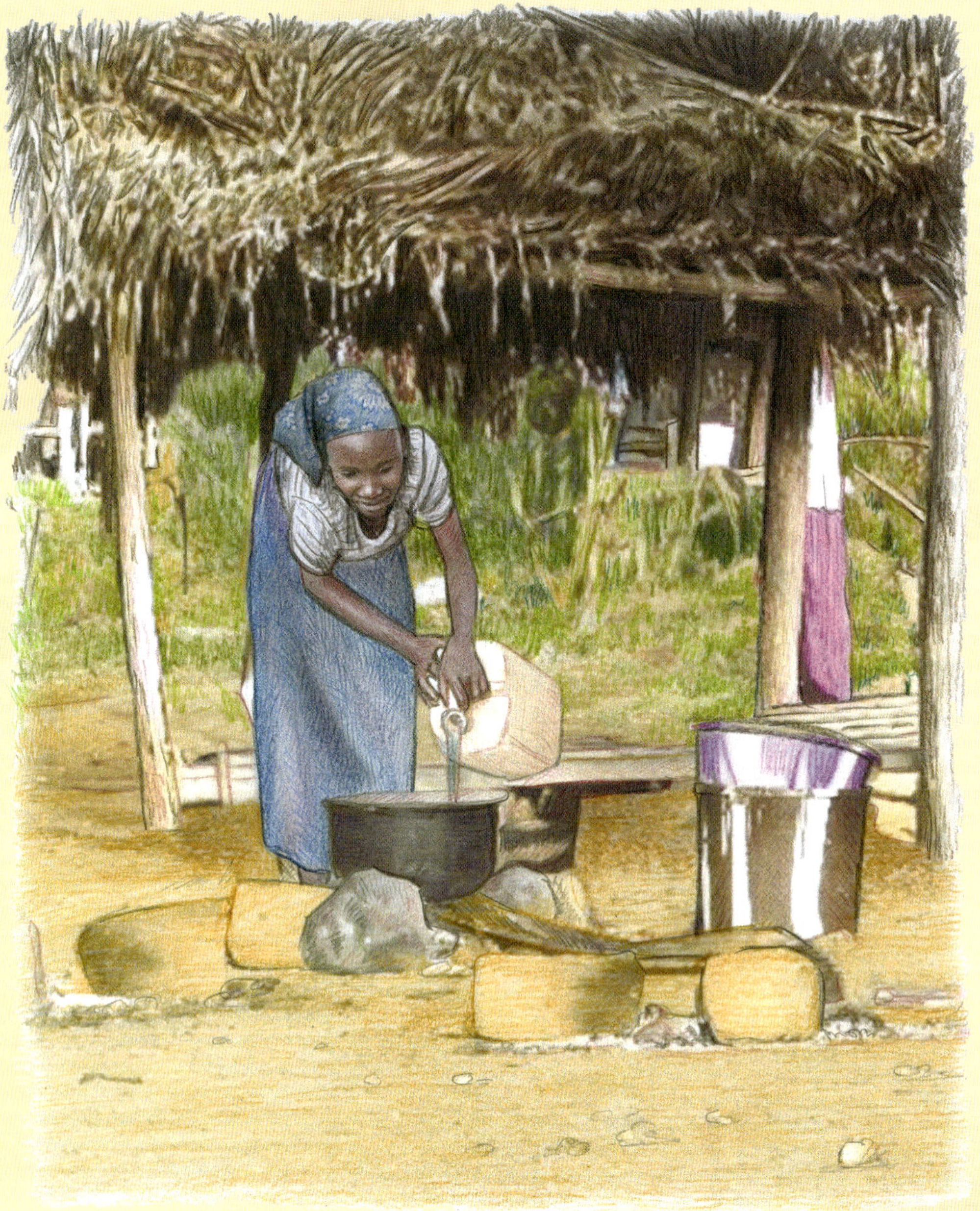

Ma lifted the lid off the pot, added some water, and replaced the lid. She fanned the fire gently before continuing.

"They gave me medicine for you and I took you along home with me that day. You were sick a few times, but you grew fat and strong. Sometimes I almost forgot you were sick.

"When you were nine months old we took you to be tested again. The nurses were puzzled. 'We don't know why,' they told us, 'but the sickness is not showing up in the test. Come back in three months and we will test her again.'

"Oh, how we prayed! When we took you back for that last test I was scared to hope. After the test, the lady got all excited. 'The sickness really is gone!' she exclaimed. 'Faith has graduated!'

"I was so excited I jumped straight out of my chair. We shouted and we cried and we thanked God that day. You were too small to know what was happening, but I think you are big enough now to understand. God DID make a way! He always does. Many people go to the witch doctor when they are sick, but only God has real power! He healed you, and I know now more than ever that when God is ready to do something, He will do it."

39

"So don't be sad, Faith. Maybe we won't eat rice tonight, but we will still eat. God will make a way. Let's pray right now." As they sat under the kitchen's thatched roof, Faith and Rebecca closed their eyes and listened as Ma talked to God. "Father God, we just want to say thank you for everything you do for us. You are good all the time. Tonight we don't have much—only this yam—but we know you are able. God, you are able to do what no man can do, so we ask that you provide for us. We ask that you care for us the same way you cared for the children of Israel in the wilderness. Thank you, God, for the answer."

When Ma finished praying, Faith felt better inside. She knew Ma was right—God would take care of them. She would eat her little piece of yam and be thankful that she did not have to fall asleep with an empty stomach. As Ma began singing softly, Faith and her sister joined in. "So-so wonder, Jesus will do it; so-so wonder, Jesus will do it. He butters my bread; He sugars my cocoa. So-so wonder, Jesus will do it."

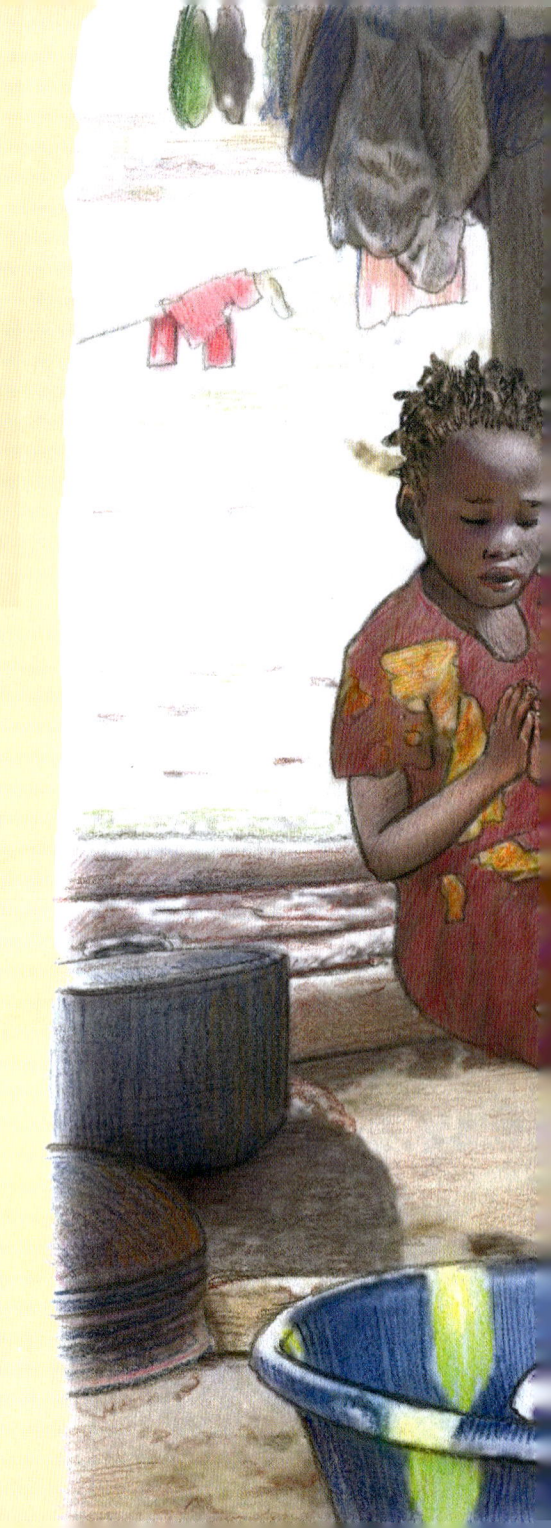

41

Just as Ma was taking the cooking pot from the fire, Faith's friend Sarah walked up. She was carrying an orange and white bowl. She handed it to Ma. "My ma said I should give this to you," she said as she skipped away. Faith heard Ma gasp. There in the bowl lay enough rice for them to eat that night.

And Faith knew. She knew God had heard their prayers. He had made a way. He always does.

About the author

A native of northeast Ohio, Melissa Wingard spent several years in Liberia, West Africa, until God called her back to her hometown. She left behind many beautiful people—people she is privileged to call friends—but the lessons she learned of the power and faithfulness of God will forever stay with her.

A teacher at heart, her hobbies include reading, writing, and spending time with the people she loves. Her desire is to use writing in a way that honors and glorifies her good and faithful Father. You can contact Melissa by writing to her in care of Christian Aid Ministries, P.O. Box 360, Berlin, OH 44610.

Author's note: You may wonder, Is this story true? The miraculous healing of the baby actually happened, and the part about God supplying food is based on a true happening. These two events were then woven into a story of an imaginary day in the life of a young Liberian girl.

About the artist

Ukrainian artist Igor Kondratyuk has enjoyed drawing ever since he was a child. As a young man he illustrated advertisements to draw people to the theater. After the fall of communism in Ukraine in 1990, Igor received a Bible. After Igor read it, God transformed him and he quit working for the theater.

Now Igor is a regular artist for CAM's *Seed of Truth* magazine. Although he rarely leaves Ukraine, his portraits have traveled to more than fifteen countries. One of his paintings is in a museum in Warsaw.

Just as the Apostle Paul made tents for a living, Igor paints. But his higher calling is preaching. He is a pastor in a conservative Baptist church. Nothing makes him happier than sharing the Gospel with others. His poor health limits what he can do, but whether preaching or painting, his greatest desire is to do all for the glory of God.

About Christian Aid Ministries

Christian Aid Ministries was founded in 1981 as a nonprofit, tax-exempt 501(c)(3) organization. Its primary purpose is to provide a trustworthy and efficient channel for Amish, Mennonite, and other conservative Anabaptist groups and individuals to minister to physical and spiritual needs around the world. This is in response to the command to ". . . do good unto all men, especially unto them who are of the household of faith" (Galatians 6:10).

CAM supporters provide millions of pounds of food, clothing, Bibles, medicines, and other aid each year. Supporters' funds also help victims of disasters in the U.S. and abroad, put up Gospel billboards in the U.S., and provide Biblical teaching and self-help resources. CAM's main purposes for providing aid are to help and encourage God's people and bring the Gospel to a lost and dying world.